THE HEYDAY OF THE SCOTTISH DIESELS

DAVID CROSS

Foreword

Title page: A scene recorded on the outskirts of Grangemouth on 8 September 1971 which typifies the heyday of Scottish diesels: Class 29 No 6121 arrives with an engineers' train as sister No 6132 leaves with a mixed freight to Cadder Yard, near Glasgow. These locomotives were built in Glasgow by the North British Locomotive Co and were later designated Class 21s; in mid-1966 both were converted to Class 29s, working for five years in this guise until October 1971 when they were withdrawn. They thus held sway around Falkirk and Grangemouth for only a short time before being replaced by Sulzer-powered locomotives of Classes 24 and 25, which would, in turn, give way to English Electric Class 37s.

First published 2002

ISBN 0 7110 2869 9

Published by Ian Allan Publishing

an imprint of Ian Allan Publishing Ltd, Hersham, Surrey KT12 4RG.
Printed by Ian Allan Printing Ltd, Hersham, Surrey KT12 4RG.

Code: 0209/A1

More than 20 years ago, when Colour-Rail was suffering the pangs of puberty and longed for the heady uplands of adulthood (now attained), it became obvious that the co-operation of real grown-up railway photographers to provide banking assistance was imperative. CCQ Color Slides had come and gone and several First Division (no Premiership in those days) senior cameramen had had their chance to refile their collections when the upstart Colour-Rail wrote suggesting that their wares might well benefit from another outing and, to their redounding credit, all three approached (Michael Mensing, Eric Cope and Derek Cross) succumbed to the bait. Derek delayed for a year, as he was, as usual, flat out supplying black-and-white prints for Ian Allan, but that did not prevent him from starting a correspondence which continued for the rest of his life (and which I have kept to this day). He had the charming habit of typing in the early hours, sitting in his Land Rover waiting for the lambs to drop (interrupted by the occasional need for physical help), and his letters were not only funny but scurrilous, abetted by his portable typewriter, which had a will of its own. A couple of keys flew off and could not be found by the light of a hurricane lamp; entirely unfazed by this, the author continued and the letter was duly sent with gaps for the reader to insert (where necessary) the missing pieces. On another occasion a black ribbon was unobtainable on an Ayrshire hillside at 02.00 so the letter was typed throughout in red ('just like my bank statement', said Derek cheerfully). Finally the shift lock resigned and politely declined to remain at its usual angle and so we had reference to @_*)_ GORDON HIGHLANDER and others, but who cared?

Larger than life, convinced that his way of running the world was rather better than that imposed by faceless grey men, Derek was wonderfully stimulating. His list of revised names for the 'Westerns' and the Class 50s was funny, irreverent and mostly unprintable, although I do recall D449 became *The Absolute End*. His ability to talk his way into (and out of) any situation was unparalleled, borne out by his dismissal of a fellow trespasser on Ducal lands by crying in his most blue-blooded tones 'GET ORFF MY LAND!', enabling him to have an unobstructed view of whatever loco might come sailing through the Drumlanrig Gorge. They don't build them like that any more, which is a pity — he was a card, and the faceless ones are winning!

Ron White
Chesham
March 2002

Introduction

Scotland, despite its size and relatively sparse rail network, was fortunate during the 'Fifties, 'Sixties and 'Seventies to have enjoyed a disproportionate number of different classes of BR diesel power. An obvious reason for this was that Scotland had no electrification aside from the Glasgow suburban ('Blue Train') network until the main West Coast Anglo-Scottish route was electrified in 1974. This meant that diesels, especially after the end of steam in Scotland in 1966/7, were the only means of traction.

Another reason was an enlightened management at Scottish Region headquarters in Glasgow. The people who ran the Scottish Region had given us a glimpse of their imagination during the 'Sixties by returning to working order four pre-Grouping steam locomotives from the Highland Railway (in yellow), the Caledonian Railway (in blue), the Great North of Scotland Railway (in green) and the North British (in brown), with enormous success in terms of public relations, railway profile and probably in revenue terms as well. The organisation was also looking for opportunities to reinforce the rail message amongst the people of Scotland. This manifested itself in different ways. Many of the early diesels that came to Scotland had had earlier spells at English sheds (the loco crews in the South West called them 'hand me doons'!); however, by accepting this power in the shape of several different classes they eventually identified the best classes and kept them. To illustrate this I recall as a 12-year-old being present at Ayr shed when two brand-new D76xx Type 2s arrived from Derby in September 1966 to replace ageing steam locomotives from that October. Managers and crews alike were very nervous because the Scottish Region had received something new — what was the catch?

Later, with the introduction of the high-speed push-pull service between Edinburgh and Glasgow in 1971, the Scottish Region again demonstrated a willingness to be bold and brave with such a new concept, and it worked with great success. It worked so well, in fact, that it was later refined with larger Class 47 locomotives and Driving Brake Second Opens (DBSOs), the bulk of which are still in use today between Norwich and London Liverpool Street.

The Scottish Region was also extremely kind to my late father Derek Cross. Every time he applied for a permit to visit a location or a lineside photographic permit (he had several for the entire Scottish Region) it would be granted. Sometimes they would tip him off about an interesting working, and often he would give them photographs, both for PR and for their own personal use. It was a strong two-way relationship, and I know it helped Derek maintain his interest in all railways after that fateful day, 11 August 1968, when the last BR steam service ran between Carlisle and Liverpool Lime Street.

Although Derek had taken pictures of diesels whilst steam was still about, they tended to be (as with some of today's steam photographers) only when the sun was out, the locomotive was clean and there was not a grubby Standard '4' to photograph instead! That philosophy, although good for picture quality, did leave gaps which I have helped fill, in order to get a good geographic spread in this book.

After his death I found a number of unfinished articles that Derek had begun. One of them, with draft title 'By Rail to Lochaber', gives an interesting insight into why he continued to take railway photographs post-August 1968. A great many photographers stopped that Sunday evening after *Oliver Cromwell* left Carlisle for Norwich light-engine, but Derek did not, and perhaps the following extract from that unfinished article gives us a clue as to why.

'To many people whose love of railways was more of an aesthetic experience rather than a means of transport, all interest in railways died with the end of steam; the newer forms of traction were dull and soul-less things … noisy, smelly and predictable. For some time I felt the same way, but a trip in the cab of the diesel hauling the 10.05am from Glasgow (Queen Street) to Fort William on 5 September changed my mind, for, though I had travelled the West Highland in the train many times in all weathers, this was something new … I saw the line as it must have been in the mind of Charles Foreman, its great engineer, when he first set out to survey it. The old Highland proverb "If you'd seen these roads before they were made … you'd bless the name of General Wade" was unfolded before me for four glorious hours, on a day of late-summer sunshine, with the threat of rain clouds to come later adding a piquancy to the experience.

Apart from the first two dozen miles to Craigendoran, this was no main line of fast trains and great engineering works; this was a line that had to use every feature of the landscape that it traversed as it twisted and clawed its way between the great hills of northwest Scotland, round the head of deep lochs of salt or fresh water or across the wastes of the dreaded Moor of Rannoch. Just as Foreman and his engineers had to use every trick they could to build the line, so the driver and his mate on the way to Fort William had to use every trick they knew to run the train to time. Modern power meant modern schedules, and modern schedules on a run as continuously curved and steeply graded as the West Highland give little time for the enginemen to sit back and admire the view. If the diesel era means that the romance of railways is dead, then it has taken a considerable time a'dying on the West Highland.

The privileged visitor in the cab of a locomotive hauling a train to the North West would have to have a heart of lead not to be thrilled by the first few hundred yards of single line at Craigendoran Junction as the coast is left behind and the single line pushes through the rock cuttings and the trees into the unknown, with only a glimpse of the now electrified Craigendoran Pier below to remind him of the urban sprawl he has left behind. The same is true on the

climb far above Loch Long, where, time and again, the line looks to be heading into a buttress of solid rock, only taking avoiding action at the last moment, the conical peak of Ben Dorain dead ahead as the train claws its way over the summit at the County March between Perthshire and Argyll; north of Tyndrum the rails dip down out of sight to the Horseshoe Bend and, above all, the Moor of Rannoch, as the last dying native pines of the Black Wood are left behind.

Such glimpses are what the 'romance of railways' means ... it was a challenge to the landscape; the fact that a steam engine might have made more noise or more smoke, been more of a challenge to photograph in view of the wind direction is all probably true, but the challenge between machine, be it steam, diesel or, to a lesser degree, electric, and the topography of the route is the real challenge of any railway.'

I think those few paragraphs give us an insight into why Derek continued to take pictures in the 'Seventies and 'Eighties. I should also like to take some credit here, because I had so much enjoyed our expeditions (and that is what they were!) in pursuit of steam traction that to stop age 14 was not something I wished to consider. I have to say that 1969 was poor in terms of photography with Derek, that being the year his farm at last got some attention. However, after a trip I made to Perth and Dundee that autumn with a friend which produced North British Type 2s and the then-new English Electric Class 50s side by side on Perth Friarton depot in nice autumnal light, something stirred in Derek. Full electrification of the West Coast main line was being considered, Class 40s were giving way to Class 50s, and the 'Claytons' and North British Type 2s had been found out. There was change all over the place, and gradually the photographic fire was re-lit.

Derek was generally well-read and had often quoted to both my mother and me a line from Kipling, who wrote in *The Day's Work*: 'A locomotive is, next to the marine engine, the most sensitive thing a man ever made.'

So, after some time off, English Electric, Crompton Parkinson, Napier, Sulzer, Barclay, Beyer Peacock and the Birmingham Railway Carriage & Wagon Co took the place of Stanier, Gresley, Fowler, Bulleid and Riddles in Derek's affections. This was just as well, because the 10 years from the end of steam (1968 to 1978) saw great changes in the composition of both traction and the railway network in Scotland. Early diesels went, new ones (such as the Class 50s) arrived and electric locomotives made it across the border to Glasgow and later Edinburgh via the West Coast main line. The Waverley route closed, and several other lines and stations were rationalised. This period was very much the heyday of Scottish diesel. Into the 'Eighties the liveries got brighter and changed endlessly, but the real variety in Scotland had already started to diminish. Nowadays, what diesels remain are of only half a dozen classes and are either red or grey.

It may come as a surprise to find in the introduction to a colour album an admission that Derek's first love was black-and-white. He liked the contrast and the challenges of getting the exposure just right and, I think, enjoyed the fun in the dark room bringing prints 'on'! Having said that, during the 'Fifties especially, getting colour film of decent quality and with remotely suitable ASA was problematic. As the 'Fifties gave way to the 'Sixties and the 'Sixties to the 'Seventies, so choice widened, and some of the greater quality is to be seen in the pages that follow.

For technically minded readers Derek's main camera was a Linhof with easily interchangeable backs and lenses and some 35mm equipment. Both colour and black-and-white material were taken on large-format negatives with eight frames to a 120-size roll film. Later, this evolved to 12 frames, in a square format, per 120-size roll. Derek used the interchangeable backs both for colour and for black-and-white photographs. The bulk of the large-format material in this book was taken on Agfa CT18 film. Later on, the Linhof was replaced by a Rollei SL66. His 35mm slides were taken either with a Leica or Canon. Much of the material was taken on Kodachrome One, because at 25ASA this was the fastest film on the market during the 'Sixties, and of good quality. Careful storage of these images, some now over 30 years old, has led to only limited deterioration and, I hope, high-quality reproduction in this book. Enjoy it!

David Cross
Brentwood
May 2002

Left: Derek Cross photographic expeditions were a family affair. Here, at Harthope in 1962, my father, brother and I watch English Electric Type 4 No D344 climbing Beattock Bank with a Crewe–Perth express. The photograph was taken by my mother, brought along to look after us children lest my father went walkabout — and to provide the picnic! Days out in the Cross household nearly always involved railway photography.

THE THAMES-CLYDE EXPRESS
1M 86
CATCH POINTS

Above left: In September 1961 'Peak' No D18 approaches Gretna Junction with the southbound 'Thames–Clyde Express', complete with headboard and correct 1M86 headcode, from Glasgow St Enoch to London St Pancras.

Behind the locomotive, the Clyde Valley line over Beattock parts from the Nith Valley line on which the train has come down from Glasgow. The Scotland/England border is no more than 200yd ahead of the train, in the middle of the bridge over the River Sark, which forms the border on to the Solway Firth. The train's next stop, at Carlisle Citadel, is nine miles distant.

At the time of the photograph No D18 had been in traffic for only 10 months, having been delivered to Derby in December 1960. (Evidently it was not just steam locomotives that were not cleaned in the 'Sixties!) It was renumbered 45 121 in February 1974 and survived until November 1987.

Left: Train 1S68 — the northbound 'Thames–Clyde Express' — accelerates out of its penultimate station stop at Dumfries in August 1963. The 'Thames–Clyde', linking London St Pancras with Glasgow St Enoch, was *the* train on the Nith Valley line north from Gretna Junction: it had priority over all others, and I can recall dilatory freight trains being shunted quickly out of the way as it approached! Although in this picture it is missing its headboard (which it continued to carry into diesel days), the 11-coach train is made up of the then latest coaching stock, has a full dining car and carries specific destination boards on the coaches.

The locomotive, BR/Sulzer Type 4 No D54, was new to Derby in August 1962 — a year before the photograph was taken — and for much of its life carried the name *The Royal Pioneer Corps*, which it received three months after the picture was taken, in November 1963. It was later renumbered 45 023 and was withdrawn in September 1984, being cut up at the Vic Berry yard in Leicester in 1986.

This page: This view taken just north of Dumfries on 6 September 1971 shows Brush Type 4 No D1747 approaching the station. In the foreground is the by now single-line branch to Maxwelltown. Prior to June 1965 this had been the start of the direct Dumfries–Stranraer 'Port Road' route, which, as the empty formation shows, had once been double-track.

Train 1M91 was an interesting Motorail service which ran daily between two points now no longer associated with direct Anglo-Scottish trains — Stirling (for the Highlands of Scotland) and Sutton Coldfield (on the edge of the West Midlands conurbation). Its make-up is also of interest, with sleeping cars, day coaches and bogie car-carrying vehicles which were themselves once coaches.

Anglo-Scottish Motorail services have come and gone over the years, with a variety of start and finish points, including (in addition to the above) London Euston, Kensington Olympia, Newton-le-Willows, Carlisle, Perth and Inverness. As a user of the service over the years I have always felt it to be a very worthwhile operation at the right price. Anything that allows avoidance of the increasingly congested motorway network is surely a concept worth pursuing.

Below: Storming north along the Nith Valley line near the closed station of Closeburn in Dumfries-shire is Brush Type 4 No 1841 with the 1S61 afternoon Birmingham New Street–Glasgow express on 21 August 1971.

The striking point about Anglo-Scottish trains then and now is how much shorter they have become. In this view we see 11 coaches including a buffet car, as opposed to this year with new Anglo-Scottish services down to just a four-coach unit. This ongoing reduction in train length and capacity makes one wonder how sincere modern passenger train operators are. How can people be re-attracted to rail services in any number when trains are half the size, much less comfortable and more expensive than they were 30 years ago?

New as D1841 in 1965, No 1841 was renumbered 47 201 in 1974 and for many years worked BR freight traffic; more recently it has been sold to Fragonset Railways and is presently in store near Wakefield.

Left, inset: One of the early types of diesel that replaced steam in Scotland was the BR/Sulzer Type 2, which later became Class 24. Here No D5009 approaches the closed station at Closeburn, some 12 miles north of Dumfries. The train is a short southbound engineers' train, which Derek records as being from the permanent-way yard at Irvine, with a destination of Dumfries. This early Type 2 diesel of 1,160hp had been introduced in March 1959 to Crewe South shed; in a working life of 17 years it had also worked on the Southern Region before emigrating to Scotland and ultimately being withdrawn from Haymarket shed in Edinburgh in July 1976 — five years after this photograph was taken on 17 July 1971. The locomotive was later cut up at Doncaster Works (as were a large number of former Scottish Region Type 2s) in November 1977.

Right: The annual Glasgow Fair holiday fortnight always saw an exodus from Glasgow to the seaside, which, in the days before almost everyone seemed to have a car or sufficient money to go abroad, meant a British resort. Some folk stayed in Scotland and went to the Firth of Clyde or the Ayrshire coast, but the great majority headed for English resorts. The beaches of northwest England had the greatest pull, Blackpool and Morecambe being the most popular.

Pictured here is the 1M32 summer-dated Saturday-only Glasgow–Morecambe train, passing through the Drumlanrig Gorge between Sanquhar and Thornhill on the former GSWR Nith Valley line behind Brush Type 4 No 1838 on 28 July 1973. The following year this locomotive was renumbered 47 188, and worked for many years as a mainly freight locomotive in England. Recently withdrawn, it presently (May 2002) resides in the scrap line at Crewe.

1M20

Left: Drumlanrig Gorge, just north of Thornhill in Dumfries-shire, is where the River Nith, the former GSWR and the A76 all come together to squeeze through the gorge. Pictured on 21 August 1971 at the north end of the gorge near Enterkinfoot is the 1M20 southbound 'Royal Scot' from Glasgow Central to London Euston. Diverted from the Clyde Valley line, then in the process of being electrified, many of the Anglo-Scottish expresses were routed through the Nith Valley. The train is hauled by a pair of 2,700hp English Electric Type 4 (Class 50) locomotives, Nos 401 and 413. Following transfer to the Western Region, these would become respectively No 50 001 *Dreadnought* and No 50 013 *Agincourt*. Neither would see preservation; although the former remains intact, after 10 years at the back of a Rotherham scrapyard it seems likely to face only the acetylene torch.

Above: Certain types of locomotive, be they steam or diesel, are immediately associated with certain routes. Often this is because the line in question is where, history tells us, they did their best work.

The whole route from St Pancras to Leeds and on to Glasgow and Edinburgh was associated with the BR/ Sulzer Type 4s universally known as the 'Peaks'. The first 10 examples (D1-10) dating from 1959 were named after English and Welsh mountains and their 'Peak' nickname was applied to the whole series, although ironically these first 10 rarely featured amongst the mountains on the Settle & Carlisle, Glasgow & South Western or Waverley routes, being instead largely confined to duties in the Nottinghamshire Coalfield around Toton depot. Nos D11-193, however, were the passenger workhorses on the steeply graded Anglo-Scottish routes for over 20 years. Pictured entering Kirkconnel station is the last of the class, No D193, with the up 'Thames–Clyde Express' from Glasgow to London St Pancras. The picture was taken on 3 May 1968; the blue-and-grey coaches in the formation indicate the move away from green diesels and red coaches had begun.

New to Gateshead depot in January 1963, No D193 became 46 056 in November 1973 and was withdrawn in October 1982, eventually being cut up at Swindon after some months in storage at Stratford in East London.

0M43
3M10
D7615

8027

Left: There was a proliferation of collieries on the Ayrshire/Dumfries-shire border, and one such was Fauldhead Colliery at Kirkconnel, which, as well as having a colliery, was until relatively recent times the only station kept open on the Nith Valley line between Kilmarnock and Dumfries. The revival of the passenger railway in Scotland during the 'Nineties has seen Kirkconnel joined by Auchinleck, New Cumnock and Sanquhar.

Pictured on 5 May 1968 are the two types of diesel which largely took over from steam in the mid-'Sixties and held sway all over Scotland for the best part of 20 years. On a short through freight from Falkland Junction, Ayr, to Dumfries or Kingmoor New Yard in Carlisle is BRCW/Sulzer Type 2 No D5348. Alongside, BR/Sulzer Type 2 No D7615, then just two years old, is on the daily trip working from Ayr Harbour to Fauldhead Colliery. After shunting empty wagons into the NCB colliery sidings the latter would return to Ayr with loaded coal wagons, Northern Ireland being the likely destination of the coal.

It is interesting to note that neither locomotive is showing the correct reporting number, one indicating light-engine and the other a parcels! Perhaps it is no surprise that use of reporting numbers on locomotives ceased not long afterwards.

Below left: It was not uncommon in Scotland to find British Rail/National Coal Board interchanges on windswept hills in the middle of nowhere! Cronberry was just such a place, situated between Muirkirk and Auchinleck on the former cross-country line from Ayr via Auchinleck, Muirkirk and Lanark to Carstairs. This line closed in stages, first to passengers and then to freight, as part of the Beeching review, the section from Cronberry to Auchinleck remaining open for some years as a freight-only branch to service the Ayrshire coal industry.

The loaded train to Ayr Harbour will depart from Cronberry behind English Electric Type 1 No 8027. The photograph was taken on 1 December 1971.

Cronberry is little more than a hamlet but was an important railway interchange serving mines at Cairnhill as well as other pits along the local river, known as Gass Water. Abandoned for many years, it was announced earlier this year that the line through Cronberry, past this site, is to be re-laid and reopened to help with the growth of open-cast mining in the Gass Water area. The Scottish Executive has allocated over £9 million towards this reopening, which will remove 3.3 million lorry-miles from Scotland's roads.

Scotland was no different from the rest of the country in that diesel shunters played an essential part in the day-to-day running of British Rail. Shunting, making up trains and even some short-haul freights formed the bulk of their work. The two pit winding wheels in the background at Highhouse Colliery, near Auchinleck in Ayrshire, confirm that No 3415 is at work preparing a coal train which later would be hauled by a Class 25 or similar from Auchinleck to Falkland Junction, the rail hub of the Ayrshire Coalfield.

As D3415, the locomotive was built at Derby in 1958. Already 12 years old when this photograph was taken in March 1970, it was renumbered 08 345 later that decade. Sold by BR in 1985, it still survives today, at the age of 44 years, being employed by Deanside Transit at Hillington, just south of Glasgow.

0S00

Left: This picture taken in early June 1963 is of Clayton Type 1 No D8539, a brand-new locomotive just delivered to BR's Scottish Region at Polmadie depot (66A) and shown approaching Brackenhill Junction on the Nith Valley line south of Kilmarnock on its way from Sheffield to Glasgow. Building of the 'Claytons' was shared between the Clayton Equipment Co in Sheffield (Nos D8500-87) and Beyer Peacock at Gorton near Manchester (D8588-8617). No D8539 spent its entire working life (June 1963 to October 1971) in Scotland, based at Polmadie shed in Glasgow, but strangely returned to England to be cut up at King's in Norwich in 1975.

Above: It is easy to forget that 30 years ago Scotland had at least two large plants manufacturing cars and vans. It is just as easy to forget that Rootes and BMC were the car manufacturers, with plants at Linwood (near Paisley) and Bathgate (near Edinburgh) respectively.

Although not much interested in politics, Derek was extremely disappointed by the impact bad industrial relations had on British manufacturing in the 'Seventies. These strikes often led to the scheduled car trains' running empty, as no vehicles had been produced for loading. Again, I recall small-money bets with my father as to whether or not the scheduled services would have any traffic. I was always the positive one, but it seems that on 15 May 1971 I had lost again, as the Bathgate–Coventry train (4M45) passes through Kilmarnock station empty! The locomotive is Brush Type 4 No D1731, a longtime Western Region locomotive which later returned to Scotland as a named ETH machine, No 47 550 *University of Dundee*.

Above: A crew change in the centre road of a large station is something we see less of on today's modern railway. However, on 30 July 1971, in the days of good old 'BR', that is exactly what was happening at Kilmarnock. A lightly loaded car train from Linwood near Paisley to 'the South', headed by BR/Sulzer Type 2 (later Class 25) No D7601, has just swapped a Scottish crew for, in all probability, Carlisle men to work the train south over the Nith Valley line to the Border City. There crews would be changed again before the train headed south to the Midlands. On today's railway, Freightliner traincrew now work all the way from Coatbridge to Crewe and back during one shift!

Dominating the background is the Johnnie Walker whisky plant. This is certainly the most famous factory in Kilmarnock, probably the most famous in Ayrshire and, some would say, amongst the most famous in Scotland! Of all the diesel renumberings under TOPS, the Class 25s' was moderately straightforward. No D7601 became 25 251 and lasted in traffic until withdrawn from Crewe depot in 1985 and scrapped at Swindon the following year.

Right: The early morning of 20 March 1963 sees English Electric Type 4 No D289 storming across the substantial viaduct just south of Stewarton station on the former GSWR main line, five miles north of Kilmarnock.

The train is the 1S26 from London Euston, the second of two heavy sleeping-car expresses that headed up the Nith Valley from Dumfries through Kilmarnock to Glasgow St Enoch every morning (the first being the 1S24 from St Pancras). In the photograph 12 coaches are in view, including some 12-wheeled ex-LMS sleeping cars, with perhaps two or three more vehicles out of sight. No D289 could have probably been heard before it came into view climbing the 1 in 75 with 15 bogies! This locomotive became No 40 089 in early 1974 but did not last long in this guise, being among the earliest withdrawals of its class, in the summer of 1976.

Below: Industrial locomotives could once be found all over Scotland, particularly in days of steam, when the mining of both coal and iron ore was at its height. However, as steam gave way to diesel and rail to road, the use of industrial shunting locomotives declined. A perverse effect of this was that industrial steam outlasted BR steam in Scotland by about 10 years; BR steam finished in Scotland in 1967, but it was the late 'Seventies before industrial steam disappeared from the NCB Waterside complex, close to where we lived in Ayrshire.

The origins of the Hunslet 0-6-0 diesel illustrated are unknown. It is pictured working for the demolition contractors engaged in the lifting of the Port Road between Stranraer (Challoch Junction) and Maxwelltown (near Dumfries). Seen in October 1968 near New Galloway station, whose signals are still in position, the green-liveried locomotive is busy shunting wagons of redundant track panels. These would be prepared for collection by a BR diesel, which would come once (perhaps twice) a week from Dumfries to collect the loaded wagons and bring further empties. Pictures of the demolition train with a BR locomotive can be seen opposite.

Right: Diesels on the Port Road between Dumfries and Stranraer were never common, as the line closed on 14 June 1965, before diesels started to take over from steam in Southern Scotland in 1965/6.

For reasons that remain unclear, the Port Road was left more-or-less intact for two years or so before being lifted. At the Dumfries end the line was lifted by starting at Challoch Junction (near Dunragit) and working back towards Dumfries. Pictured at the closed station of Gatehouse of Fleet on 10 August 1968 is one of the weekly demolition trains, this one from Gatehouse of Fleet to Dumfries Yard.

The crew of BRCW Type 2 No D5348 appear to be waiting for the contractor to complete loading their train and enjoying some fine summer weather in that remote corner of Galloway. As Derek and I were travelling with the train that day photographic opportunities were much less difficult than usual, along the lines of 'Please stop here driver — there's a shot to be taken'. This method of railway photography did — and still does — make life much easier!

5
D5340

Left: Snow on the hills in the distance gives a clue as to the season in which this picture was taken on 25 March 1966 north of Pinmore, the first station south of Girvan on the Stranraer line. The train is a Glasgow–Stranraer Harbour passenger, which would connect with the Sealink passenger ferry service from Stranraer to the Northern Irish port of Larne.

The DMU is a BR Inter-City type, introduced from May 1959 and built at Swindon. One of these sets is preserved at the Bo'ness & Kinneil Railway, the major diesel preservation centre in Scotland today.

Below: The end of steam in southern Scotland came on 3 October 1966. From that date steam ceased to work from Ayr shed (67C) and diesels took over, many having arrived only the day before! In order to get crews trained and support staff familiarised on diesels there was an overlap that lasted for two years. Pictured here six months before steam finished is proof of that overlap, with diesel and steam working together on the same train. Leaving Girvan on the viaduct over the Water of Girvan just before it enters the Firth of Clyde is BRCW Type 2 No D5366 piloting Standard Class 5 No 73145, one of the Caprotti variants, on the morning parcels train from Stranraer Harbour to Glasgow. This train was a particular favourite of Derek's (sadly I was at school!), being local and a good morning shot on the picturesque Girvan Valley line between Girvan and Maybole, close to where we then lived. The photograph was taken on 25 March 1966.

55

Left: Among the diesels that replaced steam locomotives in many parts of Scotland were 1,000hp English Electric Type 1s. These normally worked in pairs and nearly always cab-first, which gave much better visibility. It was therefore unusual to note green No D8115 working on its own, bonnet-first, steam-engine-style! The train pictured is the daily Girvan–Falkland Junction (Ayr) pick-up goods, seen on the Girvan Valley line near Bargany.

Today hardly any freight trains run on the Stranraer line. Pick-up freights disappeared long ago, but sadly, even with the modest growth in freight by rail in recent years, this arterial route to Northern Ireland has missed out.

Later in its 25-year life No D8115 made its way to England before being withdrawn from Bescot depot in Walsall in 1987 and meeting its end via the famous pyramid of locomotives at the Vic Berry scrapyard in Leicester the following year.

Above: It has to be said that Heads of Ayr was not much of a station, but such was the level of entertainment up and down the hill from the single platform there that few passengers cared. The cable-car wires in the background linked the main entrance to the Firth of Clyde beach site of the Butlin's Holiday Camp at Heads of Ayr. Ten years earlier, every summer Saturday had seen a procession of trains to Leeds, Newcastle, Glasgow and Edinburgh. By the time this photograph was taken, on 14 September 1968, the only trains were to Ayr, Kilmarnock and Glasgow.

The advent of both greater motor-car ownership and foreign holidays had reduced the rail-borne patronage to Heads of Ayr Camp, and the train photographed is the second-last train ever from Heads of Ayr — a three-coach local to Kilmarnock. (From memory the very last train, an hour later, was a DMU to Glasgow.) The train is hauled by 1,000hp EE Type 1 No D8124, at that time allocated to Polmadie shed in Glasgow and outbased locally at Ayr depot.

Left: It is easy to forget just how transport has changed over the past 35 years. In those days it was commonplace to run excursion traffic by rail over relatively short distances. Pictured on 18 May 1967 is just such an example of that traffic. Passing Greenan Sidings on the Heads of Ayr branch is an excusrion from Greenock to Heads of Ayr — a journey by road of just 54 miles along the West Coast of Scotland.

The train is headed by a clean two-tone-green-liveried BR/Sulzer Type 2, No D5053, and is just a mile from its destination at Heads of Ayr station, which was in the middle of the Butlins Camp, hence the excursion. The 'stump' from Alloway Junction to Heads of Ayr was all that remained of the former Ayr, Dunure & Maidens Light Railway. Greenan Sidings had, in earlier years, been both a coal yard and a loading-point for the famous Ayrshire 'tatties' grown locally.

Below left: In this picture taken at Ayr station on the morning of 18 June 1970, the coaching stock is perhaps even more interesting than the rest of the photograph. The train itself is a routine school excursion from Ayr to Ardrossan; 30 or more years ago it was still common for such trips to take place by rail, even (as here) over relatively short distances — business rail transport has now lost completely to road coaches. Where, however, did the green coaches come from? The obvious answer is the Southern Region, but how they got to be part of an excursion set moving children along the Ayrshire coast is a mystery.

The locomotive, which was also once green, is BRCW Type 2 No 5409, the space before the number clearly indicating that the 'D' had been removed. This locomotive was delivered new to Cricklewood in North London in the summer of 1962, migrating to Scotland in 1969. It changed identity three times, after 5408, first to 27 116, then to 27 210 and finally to 27 064, before being withdrawn (from Inverness) in 1986.

Double-heading in the Ayrshire Coalfield was not very common in either the diesel or the steam era, but there were notable exceptions: 'Claytons' and the English Electric Type 1s tended to work in pairs, and the old Caledonian 0-6-0s had earlier done likewise, particularly on the branch to the NCB coal mine at Littlemill Colliery. On 18 June 1970 two BRCW Type 2 (Class 27) locomotives, Nos 5411 and 5412, were unusually double-heading the morning Ayr Harbour–Waterside coal empties over the River Ayr at the north end of Ayr station. A possible explanation is that one of the locomotives had perhaps just had some maintenance undertaken at Ayr depot and was on test with a sister on this relatively short (11-mile) journey to Waterside, where the BR and NCB systems met.

Ayr had a large steam shed (67C) which from October 1966 became a large diesel maintenance depot and stabling point (later AY); I am pleased to report that this is still in use and during a visit in July 2001 was playing host to various modern diesels of Classes 08, 37, 56 and 66.

For many years the BR Swindon-built Inter-City DMUs provided the passenger service between Glasgow, Ayrshire and Stranraer. These three-car units, with First- and Second-class accommodation, later became Class 126. In this picture we see two three-car sets in multiple with the majority of the carriages in blue, although the fourth remains in green livery. They later became blue and grey. The train is the 2P43 Glasgow Central–Ayr semi-fast, seen crossing the River Ayr just a few yards from its destination. The photograph was taken on 12 July 1968 from Ayr No 1 signalbox.

Right: From 4 May 1970 Class 50s were introduced in pairs from Crewe to Glasgow on Anglo-Scottish expresses. With an electric between Euston and Crewe, the overall journey time between London and Glasgow was reduced to six hours. However, the reign of the Class 50s represented an interim step, because full electrification of the West Coast main line was completed in 1974. Prior to this there was much engineering work to be done, including a major bridge replacement just a mile south of Glasgow Central at the Cook Street Bridge during the last 10 days of July in 1973. This led to a major programme of diversions, using mainly the GSWR line via Kilmarnock and Dalry to join the line from Ayr into Glasgow Central.

Pictured approaching Dalry Junction, coming off the branch from Kilmarnock (the Ayr line being in the foreground), is the 1S69 Euston–Glasgow relief, headed by a single Class 50, No 439. This locomotive was later renumbered 50 039 and later still (in June 1978) named *Implacable*, following transfer to the Western Region. It was withdrawn from Old Oak Common depot in London in June 1989 after 21 years' service.

Right: With a much less flexible passenger railway nowadays, the need to run ECS (empty coaching-stock) trains has all but disappeared. However, in the heyday of Scottish diesels and earlier, British Railways had several sets of spare stock which were kept without regular work but pressed into service whenever there was a commercial need or opportunity to be exploited. Holiday traffic, soccer matches, day excursions, troop movements were all examples of irregular traffic for which coaching stock was needed.

On 22 July 1973 BR/Sulzer Type 2 No 7591 heads north near Lochwinnoch with a Carlisle–Glasgow ECS. The train has taken the secondary route from Kilmarnock into Glasgow, joining the Ayr–Glasgow line at Dalry. This section of line contains Renfrewshire's 'ghost' station. When the GSWR opened the Lochwinnoch loop line in 1906, there appeared in the working timetable, between Kilbarchan and Lochwinnoch, a station named St Brydes, 14 miles from Glasgow St Enoch station. This featured in every subsequent issue of the working timetable until 1923 at least, though no such station ever existed! The reason was that when the line was opened a project was afoot for a garden city or similar at this point, but the scheme never materialised. Travellers by this route could see the up and down lines suddenly separate to embrace the grass bank which was to have been the island platform, while the space allocated for the sidings and goods yard is also clearly visible.

Above: After 10 miles descending Beattock Bank the English Electric Type 4 in charge of the southbound 'Mid-Day Scot' from Glasgow to Euston is about to race through Beattock station, which, as well as being famous for its shed full of banking engines to assist northbound trains up the 10-mile gradient, was also a junction station. Sweeping away to the right of the train is the single-line branch from Beattock to the Dumfries-shire village of Moffat, some two miles distant.

Pictured during the summer of 1962 is locomotive D234 *Accra* (later Class 40 No 40 034), which lasted pretty much until the end of the class, being withdrawn in 1984 after over 25 years of service. No fewer than 25 (Nos D210-25/7-35) of the early EE Type 4s were named, after passenger liners, the *Accra* being one such. This batch of locomotives was allocated new to the London Midland Region in 1959.

Right: The reporting number 1S57 immediately identifies the crack 'Royal Scot' Anglo-Scottish service, whether it be 1962 or 2002. Departure and journey times may have changed but 1S57, through steam, diesel and electric, has always been the northbound 'Royal Scot'. That was very obviously the case on 1 June 1963, when English Electric Type 4 No D370 was roaring (some prefer 'whistling') out of Beattock station at the very start of the 10 miles at 1 in 75 that is Beattock Bank.

A shed full of steam locomotive banking engines look on as this then 18-month-old 'high-tech' machine sets off up the hill. The area around Beattock is geographically and climatically wild, and on the left of the picture the beautifully maintained wooden snow-fences bear out the fact that the weather in the Southern Uplands can get nasty in winter.

1S 57

Having descended Beattock Bank with a loaded oil train from the Grangemouth refinery on the Firth of Forth, service 6V56 finds itself put into the loop just north of Beattock station. In all likelihood the Class 6 freight is being 'looped' to allow a faster Class 1 passenger train to overtake.

Derek's notes on the destination of the train are incomplete, but the 'V' denotes a destination on the Western Region. Coming out of Scotland the major inter-regional destination letters were (and indeed still are) as follows: 'E' denoted the Eastern Region, 'M' the London Midland Region, 'O' the Southern Region and 'V' the Western Region.

The locomotive is Brush Type 4 No 1943, new to the London Midland Region as D1943 in June 1966 and seen here just four years later when photographed on 1 August 1970. It went on to achieve much greater fame in later life when, by now renumbered 47 500 and named *Great Western*, it was repainted in Brunswick green for the GWR150 celebrations in 1985.

Right: Anglo-Scottish expresses as we remember them and as they should be (!), with headboards, long trains and a proper locomotive. This picture, taken in the summer of 1961, shows English Electric Type 4 No D331 about halfway up Beattock Bank. The train is the down (northbound) 'Royal Scot' from London Euston to Glasgow Central, the headboard on the locomotive and the destination boards on all the coaches confirming that this was one of the crack Anglo-Scottish expresses at that time. Other trains of similar status were the 'Caledonian' and the 'Mid-Day Scot', and all three were limited to just eight carriages in order to keep to the schedule of just under eight hours.

Good photographic railway positions often change very little, but this location has witnessed two dramatic changes in the past 40 years. The first saw great forestation around the West Coast main line over Beattock, and the second, in the last year or two, has seen the M74 motorway move from the right-hand side of the railway to the left, so that it now runs across the hill in the background!

Right: The summer of 1962 sees English Electric Type 4 D231 *Sylvania* heading north with the 1S47 morning Liverpool–Glasgow express. The train is crossing the infant River Clyde, which rises nearby in the Southern Uplands. Interestingly the River Tweed rises in the same area but, of course, flows eastwards, as opposed to the Clyde, which flows westwards to the Atlantic.

Derek spent hours at this bridge, one of his favourite positions on the Clyde Valley line, and has pictures of steam, diesel and electrics taken over a 35-year period. I have been back to the bridge myself in recent years, so extending the family photographic record of this picturesque bridge over the Clyde near the closed wayside station of Crawford to over 50 years. Perhaps because of this, the bridge is now known amongst some Scottish enthusiasts as the 'Derek Cross bridge'.

1M37

Left: Class 50 No D443 races southwards along the Clyde Valley main line with the 1M37 Perth–Birmingham express on 24 March 1970. The precise location is the Lanarkshire village of Abington, where the station had recently closed; indeed, with electrification to Glasgow on the horizon, the platform faces had already been removed. The semaphore signals were still much in evidence, but these too would have a limited life, being swallowed up by the Motherwell power signalbox area. The loops at the north end of the small station still survive today, however.

The locomotive had been new to the London Midland Region for Anglo-Scottish duties in October 1968 and remained on the LMR until the arrival of the electrics north of Weaver Junction, whereupon it and its 49 sisters were transferred to the Western Region. Once there, No 443 assumed a new identity as No 50 043; it was later named *Eagle* and remained in service until February 1991. Following withdrawal from Plymouth Laira, the locomotive survived for almost 11 years in storage in South Wales with a view to preservation, but this ultimately came to nought as it was scrapped in January 2002.

Right: A pair of green Clayton Type 1s, Nos D8585 and D8571, on an engineers' train at the closed wayside station of Lamington, some 10 miles south of Carstairs on the West Coast main line. Although the station had closed by the time this photograph was taken, on 25 May 1967, the signalbox and the siding on the upside were both still in use. The guard in the 'six foot' at the rear of the train appears to be in communication with the traincrew, who appear to be using the raised cab and two driving positions to good advantage.

Members of this class of locomotive, which became Class 17, did not last long in service; No D8585 remained in traffic for just four years and five months, while No D8571 fared only slightly better, at five years and six months. Both were cut up at the McWilliam scrapyard at Shettleston in the east end of Glasgow, where a number of the locomotives featured in this volume met their end.

5M20

Left: Storming southbound across the River Clyde are a pair of BRCW Type 2s, Nos 5360 and 5331. The train is the 5M20 Glasgow–Manchester Red Bank empty vans — a working which could always be relied upon to provide great variety of motive power. This was evident on 25 April 1970, with a Class 27 piloting a Class 26 on what was always an exceptionally long train. The picture was taken south of Strawfrank Junction, near Carstairs, where in steam days there had been a set of famous water troughs.

In 1970 many of the national newspapers were printed only in Manchester and/or London, which led to a major movement of loaded newspaper vans by night and an equally large movement of empty vans back to Manchester and London by day. Today, of course, much of this traffic has gone, as technology now allows the papers to be printed much closer to where they are required.

Above: On the same day Class 50 No D438 accelerates away from the Carstairs stop past Strawfrank Junction with the 1M37 morning Perth–Birmingham express.

The locomotive was then unnamed but carried a very small oval plate where a nameplate would be, informing anyone who wanted to know that 'This locomotive is the property of English Electric Leasing' and, therefore, not owned by British Rail. So if you thought Porterbrook, HSBC Rail and the myriad of other leasing companies that inhabit the modern railway are new, they are not! Class 50s beat them to leasing 32 years ago.

No D438 later became 50 038 and would ultimately spend much longer on the Western Region than it had on the WCML. The locomotive was withdrawn in September 1988 from Old Oak Common shed in London after 20 years' service.

Above: Two-tone green, two-year-old Brush Type 4 No D1632 is pictured accelerating away from Carstairs past Strawfrank Junction with the southbound 'Mid-Day Scot' (1M35) from Glasgow to London Euston on 27 March 1967.

In population terms Carstairs is not a big town, but in railway terms it was a major junction, with lines to Edinburgh, Glasgow, Ayr and Carlisle. It once had a large steam depot, the coaling stage on the right-hand side of the picture being a reminder of the days of '64D'. When this picture was taken there was still a small depot beside the station, and several green DMUs can be seen in the station sidings behind the train.

The line branching off to the right controlled from the then Strawfrank Junction signalbox is that to Edinburgh. Carstairs was and still is a strategic triangular junction, an important part of the modern electrified Anglo-Scottish railway in Scotland.

Right: Because English Electric Type 3s (or Class 37s, as they are now better known) can still be seen on regular passenger and freight work in Scotland, it is easy to forget they were also very much part of the steam/diesel transition in Scotland nearly 40 years ago. These largely Vulcan Foundry-built Type 3s have been exceptional performers and have given great service in Scotland for a generation. Pictured passing under the magnificent signal gantry at the north end of Carstairs station, D6841 was hauling an Anglo-Scottish freight from Kingmoor Yard in Carlisle to the erstwhile Ravenscraig steel plant on the southern approaches to Glasgow on 25 April 1970. No D6841 was new to the Welsh shed of Cardiff Canton in May 1963. Withdrawn recently as No 37 141, it has now been sold to the Harry Needle Railroad Co and is presently at Barrow Hill depot near Chesterfield.

The signal gantry disappeared when the manual signalboxes around Carstairs were all replaced with the advent of the power 'box at Motherwell, this coinciding with electrification of the Clyde Valley line to Carlisle.

8S53

Sunday 15 August 1976 saw Glasgow Queen Street station closed (for tunnel engineering work) and train services to the North and East of Scotland diverted to Glasgow Central. Approaching one of the 13 platforms at this major terminus is train 5L46, an ECS working from Cowlairs carriage sidings conveying stock for a Glasgow– Aberdeen train. The use of two Class 27s (Nos 27 036 and 27 043) on this relatively easy task was probably to get the locomotives to Glasgow Central in order to take out trains later, where the incoming locomotives could not be released.

At the time of the photograph, Class 27s held sway on passenger services from Queen Street to Dundee, Aberdeen, Inverness, Fort William and the West Highland line. Although they did work passenger traffic into and out of Glasgow Central — to Stranraer and Carlisle via the GSWR line — they were not as common at this location as were Type 4 locomotives.

Because of the engineering work during August 1976 in the tunnels approaching Glasgow Queen Street, the shuttle service to/from Edinburgh Waverley was diverted to Glasgow's other major terminus. Pictured leaving Platform 1 at 'the Central' on 15 August is an afternoon Glasgow–Edinburgh train, motive power being provided by Class 27s Nos 27 101 and 27 108 (at the rear). In 1976 this platform was more commonly used for departures to London Euston or Birmingham, although nowadays trains to London King's Cross also leave from that platform as a result of electric ECML services' being extended through from Edinburgh.

The marshalling yard at Cadder was a surprisingly busy place with good photographic vantage-points at both east and west ends of the yard. Situated between Bishopbriggs and Lenzie, it was bisected by the Glasgow–Edinburgh main line, giving it two distinct halves on the same site.

Setting off westwards from the south side of the yard on the morning of 14 April 1971 is North British Type 2 No 6112. The driver looking out has presumably checked that his train of loaded ballast wagons has successfully left the sorting sidings. Its route would take it towards Glasgow as far as Cowlairs, then up the West Highland line to Crianlarich.

No 6112 lasted just another eight weeks in traffic, before being initially stored at and then withdrawn from Eastfield depot (65A) in Glasgow. It was cut up at nearby BREL Glasgow Works in June 1972.

Right: Approaching Cadder Yard in the late morning of 14 April 1971 is the morning Aberdeen–Glasgow express. The train is hauled by green English Electric Type 4 No 357. The EE Type 4 was a 'Fifties design of 2,000hp and heavy at 133 tonnes, which led to the unusual 1Co-Co1 wheel arrangement. This particular locomotive was new in 1961 to Haymarket (64B) and at the time of the photograph had just had its 'D' prefix removed and a blue data panel added. Later renumbered 40 157, it remained in traffic until withdrawn from Crewe diesel depot in July 1983, being cut up at Doncaster that October.

Below right: Passing the former North British signalbox at the east end of Cadder Yard on the same morning is the early Glasgow–Aberdeen train. Cadder, a small village which gave its name to the nearby railway marshalling yard, never had a station.

The formation of the clearly steam-heated train is unusual, with the buffet car next to the locomotive and the BSK next to that, but back in 1971 the railways of Scotland were much less predictable than they are today.

The locomotive is English Electric Type 4 No D260, the first Class 40 to be delivered new to a Scottish Region shed — Edinburgh Haymarket, in February 1960 — from English Electric's Vulcan Foundry at Newton-le-Willows, Lancashire. In traffic for nearly 25 years, largely in Scotland, it had a brief life extension as one of a small number of Class 40s taken into Departmental stock (as No 97 405) to provide power for the major project remodelling Crewe station in the mid-'Eighties.

Below: The hot summer afternoon of 4 August 1970 finds a Swindon-built three-car DMU between duties in the platform at the original station in Oban. It had come up from Glasgow Queen Street earlier in the day and would return thither in the late afternoon.

The station at Oban is dominated by McCaig's Tower, also known locally as 'The Crown of Oban'. Mr McCaig was born on the nearby island of Lismore in 1823 and purchased the battery-hill site whilst the Argyllshire Artillery volunteers still had heavy guns in position. His original aim was to build a stone wall, which was gradually extended and extended to a half-circle and later a full circle, and by 1897 this amounted to a two-storey structure. The purpose of this exercise was to provide work for unemployed stonemasons in the Oban area, which probably accounts for the stop-go progress of construction. The completed tower is 190ft in diameter and is made of grey granite. It eventually passed into the ownership of Oban Town Council in 1970 — the year the photograph was taken.

Right: Setting off southwards from Crianlarich on 20 April 1968 is BRCW Type 2 No D5361 with a Mallaig–Fort William–Glasgow train, the apparently unco-ordinated coaching-stock formation being typical of West Highland passenger operations. At 59 miles, from Glasgow, Crianlarich represents the approximate halfway point of the train's 123-mile journey from Fort William. Next stop southbound will be Ardlui (for Loch Lomond), then Arrochar & Tarbet and on to Queen Street.

No D5361 later became Class 27 No 27 015 but survived in traffic only until January 1977, being one of the earliest members of the class to be withdrawn.

SLOW

Not all the NBL Type 2s made it into Rail blue, but one such was No D6107, repainted thus when upgraded to Class 29 in early 1967. It had been delivered in March 1959 to Hornsey shed in North London. Transferred to Glasgow Eastfield shed (65A, later ED) shortly afterwards, much of its working life was spent north and east of Glasgow. Withdrawal came in October 1971.

In this view the locomotive has charge of the morning Mallaig–Glasgow service, which, in common with many West Highland trains, had frequently to wait at Crianlarich to cross a down train from Glasgow to either Oban (that branch leaving the West Highland at the end of the platform behind the train) or Fort William. Because of the length of the stop at Crianlarich, the station buffet there became legendary in terms of the quality and variety of food available. In these days of mass standardisation in buffets, it is pleasing to report that the home-made crispies and cakes were as good as ever when I had tea there, again awaiting a crossing, during 2001. Long may the Cull family keep up the good work!

I think it must have been Derek's geological training that often led him (and me, carrying the picnic and my cheap 35mm camera!) to out-of-the-way locations featuring rock cuttings, railways and roads or rivers squeezing between hills or a combination of all of these, as here in the Monnessie Gorge, between Roy Bridge and Tulloch, where the West Highland line, the River Spean and the main A86 road all pass through a very narrow gap in the rock formation.

Pictured in April 1968 is No D6103 again on the morning Mallaig–Glasgow train. The picture is made easier to date by the inclusion of the new-liveried blue-and-grey buffet car, second in the formation. During a period when buffet cars were not always available on the Scottish Region, on-train catering could instead be provided by Griddle cars, in which I always looked forward to eating — they were more spacious and offered good service and excellent food, including (on this train) locally cured Mallaig kippers.

For those of you wondering where this photograph is, it is at the old station in Fort William. In recent years the town has had two railway stations, both bordering Loch Linnhe, which can be seen in the background. The old station was pretty much in the town centre, but, in a remarkably unfriendly act during the 'Seventies, when railways rather went out of fashion, the station was moved a mile or so out of town towards the junction for the Mallaig branch, in order that a road could be built.

Pictured on 16 April 1968, with traces of winter snow still lingering on the distant peaks, NBL Type 2 No D6103 makes ready to depart with a Mallaig–Glasgow Queen Street train. The train would have run into the station locomotive-first and 'reversed' before setting off on the 123-mile rail journey to Glasgow with a fresh locomotive, in this case No D6103. It was always a puzzle to Derek as to why these generally unreliable locomotives held sway on the rugged, hostile and steep single lines that made up the West Highland lines, where the crews probably got the best work out of them during their short working lives. He always argued that more reliable locomotives would have been a more sensible choice, which, with the arrival of Class 27s and, later, Class 37s, was proven.

New housing developments and Derek Cross did not go well together, especially if some impressive railway-related scenery was at stake! However, as Corpach is one of the few towns on the West Highland extension to Mallaig that had/has any appreciable number of jobs to offer, the housing was, probably, just about acceptable to Derek! Corpach is the second station out of Fort William and has both an aluminium plant and paper mill to its industrial credit. Both over the years have provided rail traffic.

In this April 1968 view the morning Mallaig–Glasgow train is pulling away from Corpach *en route* to Fort William, where it would reverse before continuing to Glasgow Queen Street — a through journey of just under six hours. The locomotive, No D6129, is one of the few North British Type 2s that made it into corporate rail blue. Of equal interest is the full brake (next to the locomotive), clearly of LNER origin, although Derek did not record the details.

Left: Derek always used to say that spring was the best time of year to be on the West Highland line; he felt the clarity of light and the weather generally was always better and more reliable than either high summer or early autumn. This picture, taken in April 1967, would seem to prove his point!

Seen at Locheilside, with Loch Eil in the background, is a Mallaig–Fort William–Glasgow train, hauled by North British Type 2 No D6129. This locomotive, which had been converted from Class 21 to Class 29 earlier in the month, was a regular performer on the West Highland line and remained in traffic for another 4½ years before being withdrawn at the end of October 1971. Disposal followed at Glasgow Works in June 1972. Interestingly this was one of only 11 examples of the Classes 21/29 (totalling 58 locomotives) that was never stored, some having been stored three times and others once for three years — not very happy tales about a not very successful type of locomotive.

Above: This picture, taken in early April 1971 at Mallaig, shows the 13.00 Mallaig–Glasgow, hauled by BRCW Type 2 No 5356 of Eastfield depot. The large blue sign was then a feature of Scottish Region stations.

The coal wagon and the fuel tank behind the station sign confirm that Mallaig still had a freight service at the time. From memory the freight service from Fort William was not regular, which sometimes led to mixed trains of passenger and freight vehicles on the Mallaig extension — a practice uncommon on British Railways. The alternative was for the Fort William pilot engine, often a Class 20, to trundle along the 41-mile line with the coal and fuel for Mallaig.

No 5356 became No 27 010 in November 1973 and remained in traffic until 1986. It was scrapped at the Vic Berry scrapyard in Leicester — not far from Birmingham, where the locomotive had been built; the intervening 25 years, however, were spent entirely in Scotland.

Below: Classic Kyle of Lochalsh! The picturesque station at Kyle, overlooked by the mountains above the town of Kyleakin on the Isle of Skye. The locomotive is BRCW Type 2 No D5341, waiting to leave the terminus with the afternoon Kyle–Inverness train — a leisurely journey of 82 miles for this summer afternoon in 1969. At that time Kyle of Lochalsh was the terminal for the ferries which linked Isle of Skye to the Scottish mainland, and to the left of the locomotive are a large number of goods and parcels vehicles which confirm that supplying the Isle of Skye was an important part of the line's traffic.

In more recent times a toll bridge has been built between Kyle of Lochalsh and Kyleakin, and this, together with the general demise of wagon-load freight traffic, means there is today very little freight traffic on the Kyle line.

Right: The stretch of single track at the west end of the line from Dingwall to Kyle of Lochalsh was amongst Derek's favourites. His geological training and the similarity of the terrain to that on which he cut his photographic teeth in New Zealand led him to spend many days on the stretch of line between Strome Ferry through Plockton and Duirinish to the Kyle — after waiting for the sun to come out!

Because the train service was sparse, the weather extremely variable (often poor) and the local road system worse, the challenge to get good shots in good light with the magnificent Isle of Skye in the background was a very real one. Occasionally it worked, as this picture, taken on an April morning in 1968, proves. BRCW Type 2 No D5336 on the 11.08 from Kyle of Lochalsh to Inverness passes the hamlet of Drumbuie, just outside Kyle of Lochalsh, *en route* to the train's first stop at Duirinish.

It is not often that a railway photograph makes a calendar of Scottish scenery aimed at the general public, but back in 1968 this one did! 'The train in the landscape' was very much what Derek was trying to record, be it diesel or steam. He maintained his geological training had had an influence on his picture composition, and here we see the train very much as a part of the beautiful Highland landscape near Plockton station on the line to the Kyle of Lochalsh.

The train is the morning Inverness–Kyle of Lochalsh, hauled by BRCW Type 2 No D5338 — a longtime servant of the Highland lines. This locomotive is also now privately preserved and is presently being restored at Cathays workshops in Cardiff. It will hopefully reappear one day in green, perhaps even making a return to the Kyle line, where these locomotives performed so well for so long.

Right: Pulling away from a crossing at Strathcarron is an overnight Bristol–Kyle of Lochalsh railtour now on the last leg of a very long journey of around 600 miles.

The train is being hauled by two BR/Sulzer Type 2 diesels — Nos 5115 and 5132, both of Inverness Lochgorm shed (60A). These 'Sulzers' were the mainstay of the Highland-line services for many years, and the Inverness examples were easily identifiable by their headlights as evident on the front of No D5115. In the days before universal headlight provision on diesel locomotives these Highland-based examples carried headlights simply because the nature of the narrow single lines on which they operated warranted such assistance to the driver.

Below right: On 3 September 1969 the 11.08 Kyle of Lochalsh–Inverness arrives at the small Highland station of Garve. Twelve miles from the junction with the line to the Far North at Dingwall, this was a station where buses provided a connection with the much larger town of Ullapool, some 32 miles distant across some spectacular hill country along the A835 road.

The train is hauled by green BRCW Type 2 No D5333 of Inverness shed. A Highland lines locomotive for the greater part of its working life, it was renumbered 26 033 and lasted in traffic until March 1985. The locomotive was scrapped two years later, unusually at Thornton Junction depot, as opposed to one of the BR works at Swindon, Doncaster or Glasgow, all of which were involved in the disposal of the Scottish Region's Type 2 diesels.

Left: Preservation of early diesel locomotives has thankfully caught on and a Class 24 heading north out of Inverness across the River Ness could probably be just about replicated today. However, precise re-creation of this particular photograph, taken on 16 April 1968, would be impossible: the bridge on which the train is crossing was washed away in a violent storm on 7 February 1989, a number of Class 37s being marooned in the Far North as a result, and the following year a new, modern bridge opened to replace it.

The locomotive is green BR/Sulzer Type 2 (later Class 24/1) No D5132 of Inverness shed, its headlights and the tablet-catcher below the driver's window marking it out as a Highlands engine.

The train is the late-afternoon departure from Inverness to Wick and Thurso. The whole train would travel the 143 miles from Inverness to Georgemas Junction where it would divide into two portions. The train engine would normally go forward to Wick with the front half of the train; another locomotive, based at Georgemas Junction for the week, would then be attached to the rear of the train to take this on to Thurso.

Below: The railway line to the Far North of Scotland, as well as being a substantial feat of engineering, is one of considerable length. The distance from Inverness to Georgemas Junction, where this photograph was taken in September 1973, is 147 miles — just 11 miles less than from London Euston to Crewe.

At Georgemas Junction passenger trains divided, with separate portions going forward to Wick (some 14 miles distant) and Thurso (the closer, at just six miles away). The famous John O'Groats is situated on the coast between these two towns.

Seen in the platform at Georgemas Junction is the Wick portion of a train destined for Inverness, awaiting the portion from Thurso. That day the train from Thurso was hauled by BRCW Type 2 No 5341 with five coaches, two of which were BGs. Once the two portions were safely joined, the train would set off for Inverness behind BR/Sulzer Type 2 No 5116. New to Kittybrewster shed in May 1960, this locomotive later moved to Inverness Lochgorm shed, where it spent the majority of its life, working on the Highland lines; it was withdrawn from Haymarket depot in Edinburgh in late 1976 and scrapped at BREL Doncaster during the following year.

Below: This picture, taken on 15 April 1969, shows what is believed to have been the first ever visit of a 'Deltic' to Inverness. The locomotive, No D9019, named *Royal Highland Fusilier*, provides a clue as to why such a locomotive should be there. Just outside Inverness there is a large military barracks called Fort George, where, at that time, the Royal Highland Fusiliers were stationed and the locomotive was brought to Inverness in connection with a celebration the regiment was having.

Royal Highland Fusilier had arrived at Inverness piloting the morning Perth–Inverness Highland mail that day in April 1969, my father and I travelling on the train. Acceleration over the Highland line that morning was mightily impressive, with our six coaches and nearly 4,500hp!

No D9019 is one of six production 'Deltics' to have escaped the cutter's torch. Withdrawn by BR after 20 years' service (1961-81), it has now spent longer with the Deltic Preservation Society and is based at the Barrow Hill roundhouse near Chesterfield in Derbyshire.

Right: Culloden Moor, just six miles south of Inverness on the Highland main line, is not immediately famous for its railway connections but much more so for the battle there in April 1746 when Bonnie Prince Charlie's Jacobite forces, comprising mainly Highland clansmen, were defeated by Government troops led by the Duke of Cumberland. This particular battle holds a special place in Scottish history.

In railway terms the great viaduct (seen behind the train) was also more famous than the station and, because of its size and alignment, represented a photographic challenge. On the morning of 5 April 1970 Derek declined this challenge and headed for the station, through which BR/Sulzer Type 2 No D5131 is about to pass with an express from Glasgow to Inverness. The vehicles for mail and parcels, including a mail van, are in danger of outnumbering the passenger coaches!

40

5321

Left: Entering Carr Bridge station, some 28 miles south of Inverness and 6 miles north of Aviemore on the Highland main line, is a short special train hauled by an immaculate BRCW Type 2 diesel, No 5321. The locomotive seems to have been specially cleaned by Inverness depot, where it was allocated at the time. While this class has long been associated with Scotland, the first 20 examples were allocated initially to Hornsey depot in North London, Nos D5320 and D5321 being the first to be sent new to a Scottish shed. Built in April 1959 they were allocated to Leith Central (64H), the only examples of this class based there. Having lost its 'D' prefix, No 5321 would ultimately be renumbered 26 021.

The train is described in Derek's notes as 'Mr McAlpine's Special from Kyle of Lochalsh to Edinburgh'. Of the two coaches, the first is a standard BFK whilst the second coach, owned privately by Mr (now Sir) William McAlpine, was a former GER wooden-bodied saloon.

The photograph was taken on 4 October 1972, the day before Derek's birthday, which possibly was celebrated at one of the wonderful whisky distilleries that characterise this part of the Scottish Highlands!

Below: Rolling into Newtonmore station on the Highland main line with a Glasgow–Inverness express is early BR/Sulzer Type 2 No 5018. In all likelihood the train would be held at Newtonmore in order for a crossing to take place with a southbound train.

The colourful and pretty flower baskets on the platform indicate mid-summer, and indeed the date of the picture is 18 August 1973. Growing flowers at any other time of year could be difficult in a pretty inhospitable location in the heart of the Highlands some 49 miles south of Inverness.

New to Crewe shed in 1959 as D5018, the locomotive was put to store two years after this photograph in 1975 before being withdrawn and scrapped at Doncaster the following year.

Left: The station at the village of Maud, some 31 miles north of Aberdeen, was the junction of two branches which went on to Fraserburgh (a further 16 miles to the north) and Peterhead (some 13 miles due east). South of Maud Junction the line went virtually due south to join the Aberdeen–Inverness line at Dyce Junction.

In this September 1970 view we see BRCW Type 2 No D5309 arriving in the platform with a freight from Fraserburgh to Aberdeen. The freight is only two vehicles, which I'd like to think were fish vans coming from Fraserburgh, one of the largest fishing ports on the northeast coast of Scotland. Derek's notes state simply 'southbound freight to Aberdeen', but I feel sure the consist is of two 'bluespot' fish vans.

Below left: As the headboard — moderately tasteful for a railtour — so succinctly puts it, this photograph is of the 'Peterhead Farewell Excursion'. Pictured in the platform at Dyce Junction, where branches to Fraserburgh and Peterhead diverge from the Aberdeen–Inverness main line, is the last train from Peterhead on 5 September 1970.

The train engine is BRCW Type 2 No D5307, at that stage allocated to Haymarket depot in Edinburgh, and one of a series of 47 locomotives later known as Class 26. After an initial spell of use for some of the class on suburban passenger workings out of London King's Cross they all migrated to Scotland and carried out much good service, singly or in pairs, throughout the country during these years of the heyday of the Scottish diesel.

Dyce is now the station for the nearby Aberdeen Airport. In earlier days the area north of Aberdeen had a rich railway history, Dyce being almost halfway between the shed at Kittybrewster and the famous locomotive works at Inverurie.

Sitting quietly at the end of the platform on a September evening in 1970 is English Electric Type 4 No D353. The train is the 17.45 Aberdeen–Glasgow.

Southwards from Aberdeen station, towards Ferryhill, where the shed was, there were good photographic opportunities, with some impressive signal gantries, but Derek always found photography within the confines of the station itself very difficult, many of his pictures being under-exposed. This picture, therefore, picks itself, being properly exposed, in sunshine and featuring a green Class 40, a class long associated with these 'three hour' expresses to Glasgow.

The line north from Dundee to Arbroath is 'golf country', the railway shares the coastline with the golf links as well as the A930 road. Carnoustie is probably the most famous of the intermediate stations on this stretch of line, which at one stage numbered 10 in the 17 miles between Dundee and Abroath.

The real reason for the visit to Arbroath in the summer of 1969 was to see the Kerrs' miniature railway, a wonderful little set-up with some aged narrow-gauge locomotives and a bracing trip through the sand-dunes.

The DMU is a Metro-Cammell two-car set which has just arrived at its destination on a stopping service from Dundee Tay Bridge.

Right: It is said that the only passenger station on British Railways that was below sea level was that at Dundee Tay Bridge. Thankfully on the afternoon of 30 August 1969 the station was not underwater as North British Type 2 No 6112 rolled in with a Glasgow Queen Street–Aberdeen relief. Normally Type 4s worked the Aberdeen services, with the North British locomotives generally confined to trains which terminated here before working back to Glasgow. The August Bank Holiday weekend seems to have led to a motive-power shortage which has seen No 6112 entrusted with the whole 153-mile journey from Glasgow to Aberdeen. This locomotive would remain in traffic for a further two years, being withdrawn from Eastfield depot in Glasgow in December 1971. On the face of it, this meant a working life of just 12 years, but for the four years prior to its conversion to a Class 29 it was stored unserviceable, so opportunities to photograph it at work were limited.

Left: The 1M44 'West Coast Postal' was the crack mail/parcels train that ran six nights a week each way from Glasgow Central to London Euston. The 'tentacles' of that train spread all over Scotland with portions and, if not vans, trans-shipped mail and parcels making their way to the West Coast main line to meet with the main train. The 'West Coast Postal' was one of the first trains to have a time penalty associated with late arrival at its destination; timekeeping was absolutely of the essence for this important Class 1 working, even though no fare-paying passengers were conveyed. The sorting staff in the TPO mail vans were, of course, on board each way every night.

Passing through Invergowrie station, some four miles west of Dundee, is the East of Scotland portion of the 'West Coast Postal', *en route* to Carstairs via Perth and Stirling. The train, photographed on 26 April 1972, is hauled by BRCW Type 2 No 5318.

On the afternoon of 29 August 1969 a Gloucester-built DMU of 1960 vintage heads along the flat, high-speed stretch of track near the closed station at Glencarse with a service from Perth to Dundee. The 21 miles between these major Scottish towns took the local 'stopper' 34 minutes, allowing for stops at Errol and Invergowrie.

This picture proves that multi-coloured trains in different liveries are not something associated only with the post-privatisation railway. That said, green and blue units together were not common.

It is always rather sad when a once more important facility is downgraded to a shadow of its former self. Stanley Junction, where the Highland line to Inverness splits north of Perth from the direct line to Aberdeen via Kinnaber Junction, is just such a place. Prominent in the Great Railway Race to the North in the 19th century, it was looking pretty desultory on 18 September 1973, by which time the direct line had closed and all that remained was a single-line freight-only branch to Forfar, with a pick-up goods twice per week.

Pictured restarting the freight from Forfar from the single line to join the Highland line (on the left) is Brush Type 4 No 1566. Such relative superpower for an unfitted freight is a hangover from steam days, when a 'filling-in turn' was often obtained from a main-line locomotive awaiting its next booked duty, a clue to which is the locomotive's headcode, 1M69, indicating the Perth–Kensington Olympia Motorail service which the locomotive would take south from Perth later in the day. Whilst it was not required for some hours the Perth foreman has used it to do the Forfar trip, probably because of a locomotive shortage at Perth that day.

No D1566 was new to Sheffield Darnall in 1964 as one of a class which would total 512 machines. Later numbered 47 449, it is now preserved at the Llangollen Railway.

Reference is made in the Introduction to a trip to the Perth area in 1969 which I think rekindled Derek's interest in photography. The combination of fine weather at the end of August and the riot of livery colours made for good photographs: red coaches, blue and grey coaches, green DMUs, blue DMUs and (as pictured here) a green locomotive all added to the interest.

Passing the remains of Friarton shed (63A), where a blue Class 50 (No 422) and a green Class 47 are in residence, a Glasgow Queen Street–Dundee (Tay Bridge) semi-fast service, hauled by NBL Type 2 No 6116, slows for the Perth stop on 29 August 1969. Originally reclassified as a Class 21, No 6116 had been upgraded to Class 29 three years earlier through the fitting of a 1,360hp Paxman engine in place of the 1,000hp MAN original. The locomotive was nevertheless withdrawn in December 1971, from Eastfield, being scrapped at Glasgow Works the following year.

A Dundee–Glasgow semi-fast passes through the closed wayside Perthshire station of Auchterarder, two miles northeast of Gleneagles on the main line to Perth, in September 1963. The locomotive — BRCW Type 2 No D5336 — had been new to Haymarket shed (64B) in Edinburgh a few years earlier and would spend its entire working life in Scotland.

Auchterarder station had closed some years before the picture was taken. The Scottish Region passenger timetable for the period 17 June to 8 September 1963 (price one shilling, for all 388 pages!) did mention Auchterarder, but only (on page 14) under the heading: 'Passenger Train Services have been withdrawn from the following points and passengers travelling to these destinations can alight at the stations indicated and continue their journey by bus'. Passengers for Auchterarder were advised to travel via Gleneagles, some two miles distant, although the nature of the bus service between the two stations is unclear and unstated!

Derek always maintained that this should have been a photograph of English Electric Type 3 (Class 37) No D6850 and a Clayton Type 1 diesel. However, the reliability of the 'Claytons', either singly or in pairs (as seen elsewhere in this book), was so awful that 1888-built North British 'J36' No 65345 was retained in service right to the end of regular steam in Scotland. Thus on 23 March 1967 we see the three-year-old diesel and the 79-year-old steam locomotive together in the Exchange sidings at Seafield Colliery, on the north shore of the Firth of Forth.

In 1974 No D6850 was renumbered 37 150 and was later re-engined with a Mirrlees power unit as No 37 901 *Mirrlees Pioneer*. The locomotive has recently been withdrawn and currently awaits disposal at Canton depot in Cardiff.

Much less common today, an 'engine and van' was once an everyday scene on British Rail. Pictured passing Grangemouth No 3 signalbox is just such a working with North British Type 2 (Class 29) No 6132 providing the power. Having worked a freight into the docks, the combination is moving off the dock estate to return to the depot past the port authority building. The aged tug in the distance and some 1970s cars add to the interest of this simple picture, taken in September 1971.

Since 1971 the port of Grangemouth has grown successfully, with BP and the present owners, Forth Ports plc, having invested substantial sums to make it a success. It is still rail-connected, being very much part of the freight network in Central Scotland.

Central Scotland is an area rich with collieries, and one of the larger in the 'Seventies was that at Kinneil. On the southern shores of the Firth of Forth, just north of Linlithgow, it had extensive rail yards with both the NCB and BR involvement. The whole location is now much better-known to enthusiasts, the excellent Bo'ness & Kinneil preserved railway being close to the site of the colliery; if you have not already been, it is well worth a visit.

Pictured (although doing its best to remain anonymous, with the number behind the cab) is English Electric Type 1 No 8102 in late August 1971. The Class 20s (as they were later known) were built over a period of 11 years from 1957 to 1968 — a considerable time, although their demise as a class, which started in the 'Seventies, has taken even longer and is not yet complete. One of the reasons for this has been the growth of the new private rail-freight companies during the 'Nineties; Class 20s seem to be in demand particularly with Direct Rail Services (DRS), based at Kingmoor in Carlisle, where this example, in its new guise as No 20 311, survives today.

When the picture was taken on 7 September 1971, the station at Bathgate was closed and, as is apparent, pretty unkempt. Since then it has reopened and now boasts a regular and successful commuter service to/from Edinburgh Waverley. Thirty years ago it had a car terminal and the occasional mineral trains passed through, and it is one of these Class 8 coal trains that is seen passing through the station behind Clayton Type 1 No 8561.

The locomotive had only a very short working life, of just seven years and four months, having been delivered to Edinburgh Haymarket (64B) in November 1963 and being withdrawn from the same depot in February 1971 without ever being transferred elsewhere. It was scrapped at Glasgow Works in July 1973.

Below: For many years DMUs which had taken over from steam held sway on the Edinburgh–Glasgow shuttle service. However, by the early 'Seventies there was a commercial need to improve the service as well as an increasing reliability problem with the 1956 Swindon-built units. The Scottish Region took drastic action by introducing locomotives, new coaches and much-improved frequencies and journey times. This step was welcomed by customers and photographers alike. Class 27 (1,250hp BRCW Type 2) diesels were selected in pairs, one at each end of the train and recently cascaded Mk 2 coaching stock in fixed rakes of six coaches. This combination lasted for about 10 years before giving way to a further upgrade when air conditioned sets hauled by Class 47/7s with DBSOs were introduced. To complete the circle the service is now back in the hands of modern DMUs, which are functional but much less interesting!

Pictured on 7 September 1971 is an Edinburgh Waverley–Glasgow Queen Street express crossing the Almond Valley viaduct near Linlithgow between Class 27 No 5411 (leading) and, unusually, a Class 37.

Right: Push-pull trains often afford photographers two chances of capturing the same train! The demise of tail lamps in favour of electric lights also made the fact that the train was going away easier to disguise. It may, therefore, come as no surprise that in this view BRCW Type 2 (Class 27) No 5404 is about to disappear into the Mound Tunnel at the west end of Edinburgh Waverley station.

The train is one of the Glasgow–Edinburgh 'high speed' trains, as they were described at the time of this photograph — 6 June 1971. The locomotive at the other end was unusually No 7581, a BR/Sulzer Type 2 (Class 25). Very occasionally an English Electric Type 3 (Class 37) would also be used on these services as below, when one or more of the 12 specially converted Class 27s were unavailable.

15
15

2N
2N

Left: For many years the DMUs that have come to be more commonly known as Class 101s ruled the roost throughout central and eastern Scotland. These Metro-Cammell units built in Birmingham took over from steam on the non-electrified inner- and outer-suburban network around Glasgow and especially Edinburgh. Introduced from 1956/7, the last members of Class 101 are still (2002) in service in the Manchester area. Appropriately one of these old units is still painted in a Scottish (Strathclyde PTE) livery, perhaps in recognition of the good work they did in Scotland.

Pictured on 29 May 1965, this location, at Princes Street Gardens, just west of Edinburgh Waverley, was a favourite of Derek's in the spring and early summer. The unit, on a service from Thornton Junction, has just passed a sister unit on a service outward from Waverley station.

Above: Readers who take pictures will all remember a shot such as this: good light, sun in the right place, in position in good time, train arrives as planned — all just fine, except that the locomotive is wrong!

In April 1972 Derek and I had set out to photograph 'Deltics' at the north end of the East Coast main line and had lain in wait at Monktonhall Junction, near Millerhill Yard, some five miles south of Edinburgh, for the 1E11 Edinburgh Waverley–London King's Cross — all set, then along comes Brush Type 4 No D1783 (which became Class 47 No 47 302 and is still just about in traffic with Freightliner) instead of a 'Deltic'. The reaction to such an occurrence was often not to bother taking the picture at all. Happily on this occasion Derek did take the picture, thus recording that relatively short period (between steam and the present HST/electric era) when diesel locomotives held sway on the ECML.

Left: Smoking its way out of the sidings at the NCB's Lady Victoria Colliery and onto the northbound Waverley route south of Edinburgh is Clayton Type 1 No D8530. The driver and the guard are confirming to each other that all is well for the short trip to Millerhill marshalling yard on the outskirts of Edinburgh, where the coal train would work before finding its way either to the nearby Port of Leith for export or perhaps for use at a local power station.

Virtually everything in this picture, taken on 3 July 1965, has long since disappeared. The colliery at Lady Victoria Pit, the famous Waverley route onto which the train is emerging and the locomotive itself all went before the end of the decade. No D8530, although having only a short working life, also had a charmed one, being withdrawn three times and reinstated twice before finally being condemned in March 1971.

Below: Outer-suburban Waverley route as many remember it during the heyday of the Scottish diesel: green BRCW diesel with maroon stock amid the rolling green Scottish countryside, blessed with some early-summer sunshine. This Hawick–Edinburgh train is pictured in typical scenery near Heriot, some 19 miles from the Scottish capital city, having already travelled some 33 miles from Hawick on 3 June 1965. It is hauled by BRCW Type 2 No D5302, later Class 26 No 26 002.

The Waverley route lasted until 1969 before closing altogether. Recently there have been suggestions that reopening the northern end of the line would alleviate increasing traffic congestion on the approaches to the city of Edinburgh. There is also an ongoing discussion over a long single-line branch from the southern end to help with commercial timber extraction from forests in the Borders.

Below: Headcode 1S11 applied to an Anglo-Scottish sleeping-car service, which this mixed freight is clearly not; an element of laziness in evidence on the part of the traincrew of Brush Type 4 D1970 as they pass through Steele Road station at the southern end of the Waverley route. The train is in fact a northbound goods from Carlisle Kingmoor New Yard to the equivalent yard in the Scottish capital at Millerhill, just southeast of Edinburgh. The picture was taken on 25 June 1966.

No D1970 was eventually renumbered 47 643 and is presently the only preserved Class 47 in Scotland, having been based for several years on the Bo'ness & Kinneil Railway.

Right: High in the hills close to the England/Scotland border is a very long Edinburgh–Carlisle mixed freight. Both Edinburgh and Carlisle had large new marshalling yards built in the 'Sixties — at Millerhill and Kingmoor respectively — and the length of the train appears to support this decision.

The gradient post on the right indicates the train is on the downhill approach from Steele Road station towards Newcastleton, both being wayside stations on the Waverley route. One of four Anglo-Scottish routes open at that time, the Waverley route was always the most likely to close, in view of the sparseness of population along its route. This in fact happened at the end of 1969 when the line eventually closed.

Motive power for the freight on 3 September 1965 was two new Clayton Type 1 diesels, Nos D8606 and D8601. Both built by Beyer Peacock, the former had been new to Sheffield Tinsley less than a year earlier, in October 1964, while the latter had entered traffic a month earlier at Gateshead shed. The steep gradients on the Waverley route and the unreliability of the Clayton diesels combined to make double-heading essential. Two years earlier a 1937-built Gresley 'V2' would have managed on its own! To use a favourite Derek Cross expression in this regard, 'Such is progress!'

D8606

Classic *Heyday of Scottish Diesels* — a 'Deltic' on the down 'Flying Scotsman'. Emerging from the depths of Penmanshiel Tunnel, between Berwick-upon-Tweed and Edinburgh, is No 9005 *The Prince of Wales's Own Regiment of Yorkshire* on the 1S17 10.00 London King's Cross–Edinburgh Waverley. Later renumbered 55005, this longtime Gateshead locomotive would remain in traffic until February 1981, when it was withdrawn from York depot. It was cut up at Doncaster in 1983.

As well as recalling the details of the train I also remember the date — 10 June 1972. I had been having nightmares about my A-levels, and the Derek Cross solution to his son's apprehensions was to spend the Saturday before the exams began out photographing on the East Coast main line. We had a most enjoyable day in good weather, and as well as the 'Deltic', captured Class 47 No D1500, a Class 37 on a passenger and a Class 40 on a Freightliner — and, in case you are concerned, I passed my three A-levels!

Front cover: Passing across the famous golf links north of Troon and entering the junction station at Barassie is a Class 8 unfitted train of coal wagons returning empty from one of the Glasgow power stations to Falkland Junction, the main marshalling yard for the Ayrshire Coalfield.

The locomotive is No D8525, one of the Clayton Type 1 diesels which were not a great success and had very short working lives — just eight years, in this case. It was withdrawn from Polmadie shed in Glasgow in June 1971 and cut up four years later at King's scrapyard in faraway Norwich.

The photograph was taken on 22 June 1966 — four months before steam ended in Ayrshire. The 'Claytons' had earlier been tried on the steeply graded colliery branches, normally in pairs and sometimes with a brake tender as well, but the trials were unsuccessful and 30-year-old steam locomotives held sway on the branches. The line from Ayr to Glasgow is much less challenging, and it was thus no surprise to see the 'Clayton' employed on this duty.

Back cover: In the spring of 1965 an unidentified (but probably No D309, according to Derek's records) English Electric Type 4 (later Class 40) is pictured at Elvanfoot, in the Clyde Valley, with a service from Glasgow Central to London Euston. In less than a decade this scene would be radically altered with the arrival of the 25kV electrification.

Elvanfoot was the junction for Wanlockhead, but this line was long gone in 1965, having closed prior to the outbreak of World War 2. Note the Clayton on a pick-up goods in the background, above the express's first and second coaches.